Crochet For Beginners:

A simple beginner's guide to learn easy modern crocheting, with patterns and stitches. How to realize beautiful creations and discover amigurumi techniques.

Contents

Introduction

What do Eva Longoria, US President James Buchanan, Debra Norville and Madonna have in common? Crochet. Believe it. Debra Norville even has her own yarn line. These are just some of the people who have been hooked on crochet (pun intended).

Crochet is one of the oldest forms of craft. It has also been one of the main methods in creating clothing for thousands of years. Crochet is basically creating fabric and clothing from yarn and thread with a hook.

The History of Crochet

There isn't an exact date when crochet started. It has been mentioned throughout earlier times. Experts claim that this craft has been around as early as 1500 to 1800 BC. Basing on the hand technique of basic crochet, it is presumed to have originated in the Middle East. Some claim that crochet actually originated in China and only spread to its neighboring countries such as the Middle East and eventually to Europe.

Crochet became most notable when French nuns started to crate elaborate and delicate patterns. They were known to create complex lacework using very fine materials. They made table clothes used to cover the altar and adorn the church. It was said that the art of crochet was a closely guarded craft among the nuns. It became an integral part of life in the convent.

Over the years, crochet found its way to Scotland and England. From the nuns, the knowledge and skill were passed on to the upper class. Crochet circles were established among the ladies of the upper class. The work was no longer focused on delicate and complex lace but was just as elegant. During those times, the skill was limited among the upper class. The poor were not given the privilege to learn the craft.

During the Renaissance, both the upper and lower classes were practicing crochet. During this time, the ladies were using macramé, which is several fine threads knotted together. They made delicate lacework which became popular across Europe.

In the 1820s, crochet was introduced in Ireland. They used fine threads and made delicate work that imitated English lace. It became known as Irish lace. Over the years, Irish lace became very popular in Europe, especially in the Balkans.

By the early 1900s, yarns changed from fine threadlike materials to something much thicker. Hook sizes also changed in order to accommodate the thicker yarns. Patterns started even more simplified, a deviation from the complex lacework in last years. Crochet items progressed from lacework such as table covers and church adornments, into something more practical such as gloves and scarves.

Modern Crochet

Today, crochet skills are too simple compared to how the French nuns used to make them. The craft has become widespread, but the skill levels can be compared to the level of primary school crochet.

It is still considered fabulous but way below the level that crochet used to be.

Also, compared to decades ago, there are considerably fewer people who are interested in the craft. Learning the skill is no longer confined to closed groups, but fewer people are willing to try. Mass production and cheaper goods have made people less inclined to making their own socks or blankets.

However, there are still a considerable number of people who keep the skill ever evolving. There are still people who wish to learn the craft.

Today's patterns are simpler. Popular ones include baby items such as sweaters, socks, bonnets, booties and blankets. Other items include Afghans and adult wear such as scarves, socks and sweaters.

Knitting vs. Crochet

Crochet is often confused with knitting. They are closely related but very different in ways, too.

Common elements:

The following are common elements between knitting and crochet, which often creates the confusion between the 2 crafts:

- Both knitting and crochet use yarns and other similar fibers.

- Both crafts create similar items such as sweaters, blankets, Afghans, wraps, hats, socks, mittens, shawls, and scarves, among others.

- Both base projects on patterns that use abbreviations. Some abbreviations are even the same in knitting and crochet.

- Skill sets are similar between the two, which includes good hand-eye coordination, affinity for fiber, a good eye for design and color and patience to see a project through.

Differences:

The main difference is on the supplies used. Knitting can use knitting needles, knitting looms and knitting machines. Crochet uses only one for all projects- a single crochet hook. The hook sizes determine how big the stitches turn out to be. Crochet has always been made by hand. The movements in crochet are so elaborate that it has yet to be replicated by a machine.

Another difference is the structure of the fabric made. While both crafts involve manipulating loops, how the loops are built differs. In knitting, the loops are built on top each other. Several loops are active at the same time, held in place on the knitting needle. One dropped stitch can cause an entire column of stitches to drop. In crochet, only a few loops are active at the same time. The stitches also build on top of each other, but the active loop is only limited to a single pot. This way, a dropped stitch will not cause a bunch of stitches to unravel.

Chapter 1

Types of Crochet

Amigurumi Crochet

This type of crochet is said to have originated from Japan. People would use this type of crochet when making toys that would be stuffed using this crochet. Ami means knitting or yarn that has been crocheted while amigurumi means a doll that has been stuffed. This type of crochet is therefore used when one is making these stuffed dolls through the use of heavy yarn. One can also make fan items and the large novelty cushions as well as the homewares.

Aran Crochet

This is a type of crochet that is normally ribbed and also one that is cabled. It is a traditional type of crochet which is made through interlocking cables. Through this type of crocheting, one can make sweaters and chunky beanies as well as scarves. This type of crocheting is said to produce very strong items as a result of the interlocking of the cables. This is the reason why people use it to make items that would need to be worn for longer periods of time. They can also be used to make blankets and aphgans as well as jackets and coats and also scarves.

Bavarian Crochet

This is a type of crochet which is said to work just like the granny squares, which were traditionally made. It is used when one wants to make very thick items and also when they want to blend in different colors when making them. This type of crochet is said to allow people to be able to blend in different colors without experiencing any challenges. They are able to do this by working on each part on its own. This helps them to be able to blend them together, which makes them come up with a very fancy item. The granny squares make it very appealing since one can even use squares of different colors. One can make blankets and shawls through the use of Bavarian crochet.

Bosnian Crochet

Bosnian crochet is used when one wants to make a dense and knit like materials through the use of a crochet slip sew up. One has to, however, stitch different parts of a stitch on the current row. One has to ensure that the stitches are different in each row. They are able to achieve this through the use of the Bosnian crochet hooks, which are said to produce very good crochets. One can still work with the normal hooks; even the Bosnian hooks give better crochets than the other hooks.

This type of crochet is not very popular. This is because one would think that it is normal knitting when you look at the crochet. It is easy to work with it since the style used is easy to learn. People use it when one is making the scarves and beanies, as well as when crocheting items that do not require much time to be crocheted.

Bullion Crochet

This is a type of crochet that requires one to use a lot of time when making them. One uses many wraps of the yarn, which have to be put around a hook that is very long. By doing this, one is able to come up with a very unique stitch. This type of crochet is used when one needs to make the motifs and not when making crochets that require one to use the fabrics.

It takes a lot of time to produce the item you are making using this type of crochet since one has to be very keen when coming up with the patterns. The final product is normally very firm and thick, as well as stiff. A crocheter uses a method to make items that are meant to be long-lasting. One can make mats and stiff materials when they use this type of crocheting. This helps them to be able to come up with materials that are very unique and firm, so they can be used for a very long time without them wearing out.

Broomstick Crochet

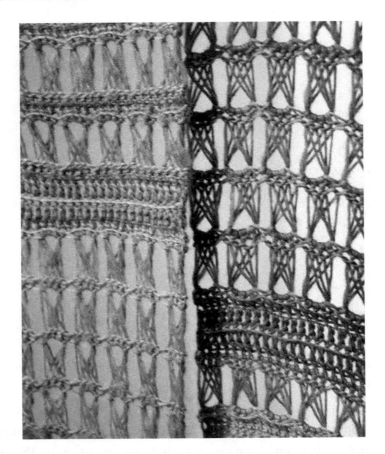

This type of crochet is also called jiffy lace. It is normally made through the use of traditional crochet hooks. One form makes some stitches all round a very long as well as wide stick that looks like that one of a broomstick. In this modern age, people are said to use the large crochet hooks as well as the thick dowel when they are making the broomstick lace nowadays. It is a skill that people need to take their time to learn in order for them to come up with a well-made crochet. It is, however, a type of crochet that is said to produce crochets that are very beautiful and unique. One can make baby shawls using this type of crochet and also throw blankets that are normally used for the purposes of decoration.

Bruges Crochet

This is a type of crochet that is used when one wants to make Bruges laces, as the name suggests. One first creates ribbons meant for the crochet, which are sewed together in order for them to form the desired lace pattern. They are said to form very beautiful patterns that are also unique. This is because they are neatly sewed together. One can use different colors when making these patterns, which makes them even more beautiful. This type of crochet is used for making table mats and shawls as well as embellishments that are used for clothing.

Clothesline Crochet

This is a type of crochet which is said to utilize the stitches that were used traditionally. One uses a very thick yarn when making items using this type of crochet. They work on a rope that has to be very thick since when making mats, one requires something that will be so strong, and which will be easy to style as well as shape. This type of crocheting is mostly used when one is making mats and baskets or anything that is required to be strong. One needs to have skills on how to make items using this type of crochet since they need to make first make the item they need to make on the ground before they can crochet it. This type of crochet is used in the making of mats and baskets as well as wall hangings.

Clones Lace Crochet

This type of crochet was said to be easy to make in the past and was very popular among people who love crocheting. It resembled the Irish lace, which was made because it was so easy to make. Clones knots are made, which makes as they are normally part of the crocheting process. One needs to learn this skill in order for them to ensure that they know how to make items using it. This type of crochet is used when one is making delicate dresses that require one to be very keen.

Cro-hook Crochet

With this type of crochet, one is required to use a hook that is dou-ble-sided in order for them to be able to achieve crochets that are dou-ble-sided. The crocheter is expected to work on an item from both sides. He or she can work from either side of the item, which enables them to come up with a very unique pattern. It is important for a crocheter to be able to learn this style before using it to male items in order for them to get good out of the outcome from it. One can make baby clothes and scarves as well as washcloths through this type of crocheting.

Filet Crochet

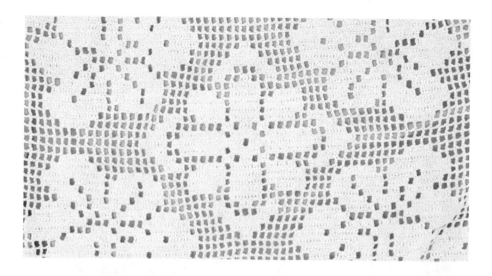

This crochet is a style that is achieved through the use of chains as well as double crochets. One achieves a crochet that has a pattern that is grid-like, which can be filled or left without filling. The space that is left is used in the creation of desired pictures which have to be included in the design. It creates patterns that are so unique and are neatly embedded within the crochet. This is something that is so unique about this type of crochet. All the squares that are left empty when crocheting may be filled with pictures of one desire. This type of crocheting is used when one is making the baby blankets, handbags, jackets, and kimonos, as well as when they are making cushions.

Finger Crochet

Finger crocheting is practiced when one barely uses the hook when crocheting. It is used when one is making some hand fabrics. During this type of crocheting, one will mostly use their hands to crochet. The patterns are fixed together to come up with one complete item. When one is making fabrics using this type of crochet, one cannot do it too fast. They will spend a lot of time crocheting, which may make them make very few items for a very long period of time. One can only make some string bags and small scarves which do not require much time when making them.

Freeform Crochet

When making this type of crochet, one does not create any pattern on the item. It is crocheting that very artistic in nature and also very organic. Crocheter does not follow any plan, so one can come up with any kind of design that they would want. There are, however, people who do not like this type of crochet since they cannot do it without any kind of plan. They need to follow some instructions in order for them to be able to make their desired patterns. One can make art pieces using this type of crochet. They can design anything that they desire to design.

Hairpin Crochet

This is a type of crochet which is said to work just like the broomstick crochet even though in the past, people used crochet hooks. Pieces being crocheted were held together through the use of metals that were then. One is able to get very beautiful and unique crochets which are well finished. They are used when one is making shawls and wraps as well as scarves.

Micro Crochet

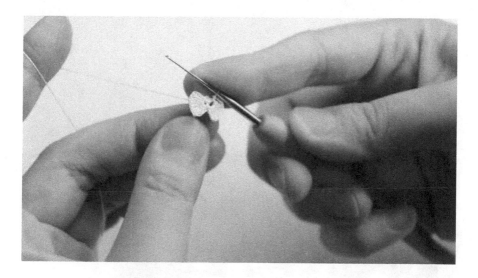

Micro crochet is used by the modern woman to make crochets. They make use of threads that are very fine and crochet hooks that are also very fine. A crocheter has to make sure that they are very careful when using the hooks in order to ensure that they use them in the right way in order for them to make the best types of crochets. They are used when one is making the talisman and embellishments as well as when making teeny tiny things.

Overly Crochet

Overly crochet is used when one wants to achieve an item that has stitches on top of the item, which enables them to be able to get a pattern that is raised. One can use more than one color when crocheting, which will enable them to be able to achieve unique and beautiful patterns. They can also make different designs using this type of crochet. One can use this type of crochet when making potholders as well as wall hangings as well as handbags.

Pineapple Crochet

When making items using this type of crochet, one does not follow any given pattern. This is because one can use just one general stitch, which they use to shape their desired patterns. One can use the pineapple when making these patterns. They use it to make scarves and shawls as well as wraps. This type of crochet is not complicated since anyone can learn it and be able to crochet items into their desired designs.

Chapter 2

***

Crocheting Supplies: Tools and Materials

Here are the basic materials for starting up a crochet project:

- Yarn

- Crochet hook

- Scissors

- Darning needle

- Tape measure

- Hook organizer

- stitch markers

- Row counter

- Stitch patterns

- Crochet material organizer

The materials help in one way or another in making crochet. However, for beginners, one can use the basic ones.

Yarn

Yarn is a thread used in sewing or knitting any form of material. This is the backbone of crochet. It is the only material that comes out of the final product as it carries everything from designing to the conclusion. For beginners, it is advised to use a medium weight yarn as it is easy to crawl it with the hooks.

There are different types of yarns according to your preference and it is better to understand them before buying. The common material is polyester and wool. There is also nylon, acrylic, rayon and viscose which can be the best choice according to one's preference.

Here are the types of yarns:

- Natural fibers

- Synthetic fibers

- Eco-friendly fibers

Natural Fibers

These are yarns made from natural materials.

Cotton

This is a material harvested from cotton plants a process is used to preserve them to last longer.

Silk

This is form of material made from the larvae of silkworm and is mostly incorporated with other fibers to create a neat and long-lasting yarn.

Cashmere

Just from its name, you can see it is drawn from a cashmere goat and is known for being soft and warm at the same time.

Linen

This is harvested from a flash plant and is commonly used for light garments.

Wool

This is so common in clothes and yarn and it is a perfect material for heavy yarns.

Synthetic Fibers

As stated above, this is the commonly preferred materials for yarn and is among the selling materials in the world. This includes nylon, polyester, acrylic, rayon, and viscose.

Eco-friendly fibers

Organic Cotton

This is cotton made from cotton plants and is not treated with chemicals.

Bamboo

Bamboo has always created many products for different uses and its silk is harvested as it makes a perfect yarn because of its strength.

Those are just a sample of the commonly used yarns which are formed from different fibers for different types of crochets according to users' need.

Hooks

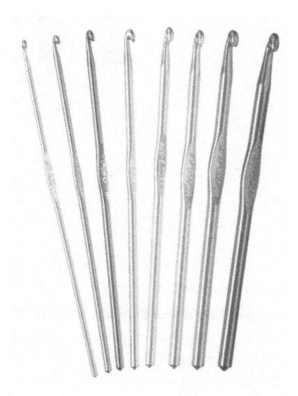

This is primarily the needles used to hook up and do stitching on yarn to form crochet. The hook drives the yarn on each one in a back and forth manner to form beautiful crochet. Sometimes, it is used concurrently with needles when a misstep is made on crochet.

Hooks come in different sizes and it is better to choose a perfect one depending on the yarns' sizes and design. It is advisable to always consider all these before starting up for some hooks may not perfectly fit your desired project.

Scissors

This is a tool commonly used in homesteads for homemade clothes or trimming of oversized curtains and towels. It is also known for being used by tailors for cutting their materials and another trimming of textile. Scissors on crochet are also paramount.

Just like the hooks, the scissors have its types and different functions on a craft or any material using yarn and hooks. The basic one is the general craft scissors which can be found locally and easily. It is okay to use the general craft scissors on different fibers because it does not leave sharp edges and cuts in a zigzag manner just like the pinking shears. Here, the type of scissor does matter when the crochet is in the completion stage as it helps cut it into nice pieces without producing threads and tears inappropriately.

When buying them online, make sure you check their specifications, as others might not be suitable for your project. The recommended scissors are standard, snips, embroidery scissors, and lastly the dressmaker. Embroidery scissors could be perfect for this case because it helps cut the exact yarn being used without tampering with the rest of the project.

Darning Needle

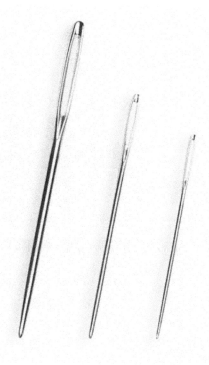

As the name suggests, it is a form of a needle with a bigger hole than the normal needle where the yarn passes through. The sharp end is a little blunt compared to a sewing needle and helps in making a perfect end on crochet. The darning needle is used to fix the end of each crochet to enable it to stay stable when in use. This is similar to sewing where you tie a knot in the end of the material, but for crochet, the darning needle is used to make the knot, which will keep the whole crochet intact and in perfect shape.

There is no big problem when choosing a darning needle as one can compare with the size of the yarn and its hole to see if it perfectly fits. The one with a larger hole can accommodate every kind of yarn and there should not be any problem whatsoever.

Stitch Markers

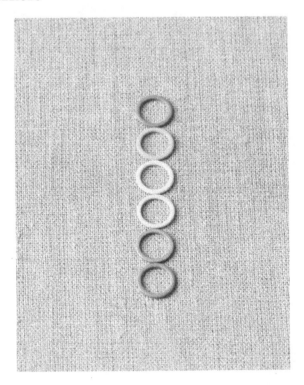

These are clips used to mark areas of interest in crochet. There are different designs of crochets and when you have a slightly complex craft; it is always advisable for one to have a stitch marker. For beginners, it is always complicated to make crochets with corners or even rounded by following the pattern. This means the stitch markers are perfect for making areas where it forms patterns unless one is a professional.

Stitch makers have crafted clips that help indicate or put marks on a design to help a beginner or a craftsman to have a perfect and uniformed crotchet.

Any size and type of stitch markers can be used on any piece and type of yarn, as it does not favor the material. The maker can be found in local stores and most people prefer them depending on the sizes of their hands, or how perfectly they can hold them.

Tape measure

Some of you could be wondering why almost everything that is used by tailors is being used to craft crochet, and the answer is yes, it needs to be totally perfect. Tailors are always seen with tape measures and to make crochet, you might want to get one too, especially for a beginner. The tape measure is simply for measuring and making the right adjustments when following a designed pattern.

This is a necessary tool when there is clipping using stitch markers as it will help to create uniform patterns and with minimal or no blundering.

However, for crochet flowers, this might not be necessary as they are very simple and can be modified easily, but it is advisable for big projects and to avoid disappointments at the end of it with different and unorganized sizes.

Tape measures also come in different sizes and types and other specifications depending on the country you are located in. For a clear understanding, make sure you get a tape measure that supports your form of measurements. For instance, America's measurement is different from Russia's and the United Kingdom. To make perfect measurements, beware of the measurements placed as some may be misleading or have different calculations depending on their form of measurements.

Stitch Patterns

These are the format you at achieving at the end of your projects. This can also be found in tutorials of some craft enthusiasts who have knitted samples of crochets and might be a good chance to get out of your comfort zone and learn some styles or even create some at the end of the day.

For a specific stitch pattern, one can learn their way through and come up with perfect crochet by just following the simple rules. Listed below are some of the common stitch patterns for beginners and can be useful for your first project.

i. Twist headband

These are perfect headbands one can make in one day for beginners. The twist headband can be put on the head and is perfect for the ladies to help hold their hair just like a clip. Unlike Marvin, it only covers a quarter of the hair and is comfortable and perfect for the winter season. This can be a good project for beginners.

ii. Marion's Cozy Mug Warmer

Crochets are not only for wearing but for beauty; it is a craft and can be used in many forms. As the name suggests, this is a cover for a mug and is good for cold seasons. This is a unique design and also simple for beginners who are looking forward to creating beautiful designs.

Iii. Snowflake Patterns

Nothing is as perfect as a snowflake and its design is even mind-blow-ing. It may look like a tiny piece but when done, it is perfect crochet that can be made with easy steps. They can be used to beautify the house or even create designs in clothes.

iii. Jingle Bell stocking

When you hear the word jingle bell, what rings in the mind is not a bell but Christmas, yes, the stockings are made using yarn and it makes a good crochet for a beginners' project. They are made to look like the Christmas attire for Santa Claus and can be spiced up by using red and white color.

With these stitch patterns, one can create a lovely design for beauty purposes or even gifting a loved one. A beginner should always keep an eye on the prize, which is the ultimate pattern that will be a result of the design.

Hook Organizer

After making the first and second pattern, you get to know the stitch patterns and designs that can work for you as you continue to be creative and innovative. The hook organizer resembles a toolbox for a car which is always referred to as Do It Yourself and can work on your car anytime, anywhere. For the crochet, this is almost similar as it carries your essential materials for the work.

After finishing the work, the hook organizer helps keep all the materials used as it has pocket-like spaces for placing hooks, tape measure, darning needles, yarn and other combinations of crochet tools. One can make any design that can hold the materials with ease and keep them in order. Instead of buying a toolbox for such materials, make one to be among the projects and you will be shocked at how you continue to perfect your craft.

Chapter 3

***

Crochet Terminology

You now know the basics of crocheting, and you're ready to move on to something a little more complicated. Before you do though, you'll need to learn the numerous abbreviations that are used in these patterns so that you can read them correctly. These terms will be used in this for the patterns as well, making sure that you get used to them to help you move forward.

The first thing to know is that the UK and the US do label stitches differently, so you'll need to know where it comes from if you want to understand your patterns properly. You'll find an easy conversion chart below.

UK		US	
Chain	Ch	Chain	Ch
Slip stitch	Ss	Slip stitch	Ss
Double crochet	Dc	Single crochet	SC
Half treble	Htc	Half double	Hdc
Treble	Tr	Double	Dc
Double treble	Dtr	Treble	Tr
Triple treble	Ttr	Double treble	Dtr

Skip a Stitch:

This means that you'll miss your following stitch. You will continue with the following one after the stitch that you've skipped.

Dc2tog:

This is an abbreviation that means you need to put two double crochet stitches together to form one stitch. To do this, you'll need to put your hook into the following stitch, and then perform yr (yarn over), and then draw it completely through. Don't finish the dc (double cross) stitch. The hook will then need to be put into the following stitch, yr, and then pulled completely through it. This will put three loops on your hook when done correctly, and then yr to pull them together.

Foundation Chain:

A foundation chain will be your base chain and you'll add stitches on top of it. This is what you'll work all of your following stitches back into.

Foundation Row:

This is a little different than a foundation chain, as it's the row that you're working into the foundation chain.

Turning Chain:

You've already learned how to turn a chain, and turning chain refers to the stitches that you're using as extras to work with at the beginning to create the new row. It'll bring you up to the proper height to start the following row. Different stitches can require different numbers of these stitches to work properly.

Dc3tog:

This is commonly called the cluster stitch. This is where you work three of your dc stitches into one, and you'll be working with the three stitches in a row, but it'll result in four loops being on your hook. Yr., drawing it through all four

Acrylic: This is a synthetic yarn, which is why it is more affordable.

Black Loop Only: This is where you'll focus only on the back loops that you are making.

Back Loop SC (Single Crochet): This is another variation of a SC stitch, which will focus on just the back loops when making it.

Color Flashing: This is seen in many patterns, and it's an effect that happens if you're using a variated yarn. You'll have unintentional patterns show up in your work, which will create unique patterns.

Coned Yarn: This is a yarn that has been wound onto a holder that is cone shaped, and it's often easier to work with as you move on to more complex patterns.

Floats: When crocheting, there are some unused pieces of yarn, or rather strands that will be carried onto the back of the project.

Frog: This is used as a verb in crocheting, such as "to frog". It is to rip out your stitches. This will add decorative or functional pieces. This can be used for when you're adding buttons.

Freeform Crochet: This is where you aren't crocheting from a pattern, and this is great when you're practicing your stitches. You explore the craft, and you'll usually end up with a unique pattern.

Granny Square: This is a crochet pattern that is just made of a simple ring of chain stitches, and then you build on it outward. They are often put together to make a blanket.

Inelastic: When you're working with an inelastic yarn it won't recover its original shape quickly if at all after you've stretched it.

Kitchen Cotton: When you're looking for a yarn that's easy to use and useful in projects, you'll want to find kitchen cotton. You can use it for placemats, potholders, and even dishcloths.

Pjoning: Once you know how to use ss (slip stitch) easily, you'll be able to move on to a pjoning, which is where you use it to create different, unique fabrics.

Plarn: You'll find this when you're shopping for yarn, as it's a plastic yarn. It's often recycled, where bags and other plastic items were cut up and repurposed.

Place Maker: You'll want to use these when you have to stop a project, and it's where you mark it in a way that you can remove so that you don't lose your stitch. Many people will use safety pins that can easily be taken out.

Protein Fiber: This is a fiber made from protein, but it's not something a beginner should be using.

Scrapghan: This is where you make an afghan, which can be put together through granny squares or granny triangles, but you use your yarn Scraps to make it. This will often have a large variety of colors and yarn types.

Shell Stitch: You'll learn this as one of your last stitches, and it's where you've looped multiple stitches into a single one.

Tapestry Needle: This is a sewing needle that is often used in embroidery.

Variated Yarn: This is a yarn that has a variety of colors, allowing for unintentional patterns of color to appear in your pattern.

Self-Striping Yarn: This is a type of variated yarn, and it has two or more colors in it. It usually does not change colors quickly, so you'll have long stretches of each color. You can get some variegated thread that has a shorter stretch of each color.

Work Even: This is your goal with most patterns, especially as a beginner. You'll want to continue in the same stitch pattern. You do not want to increase or decrease.

Worsted Weight Yarn: You'll find this in many simple patterns, and it just means a medium weight.

Yarn Cake: This is a method that you use to wind yarn.

Abbreviations:

Beg- beginning	Hdc- half double crochet	Sp(s) – space(s)
Bg- block	Htr – half treble crochet	St(s)- stitch(es)
Cc- contrst color	Inc- increase	Tog- together
Ch- chain	Rep- repeat	Tr—treble crochet
Dc- double crochet	Rnd- round	Tr tr- treble treble crochet
Dec- decrease	SC- single crochet	Ws- wrong side

Dtr- double treble crochet   Si st- slip stitch   Yo- yarn over

[ ] = work instructions within the brackets. Do this as directed

( ) = work within the parentheses as the instructions direct you. It'll tell you how much to do so

*= repeat what instructions followed the single astrix. Follow the directions

**= repeat the instructions that followed the double asterisks, as directed and so on

Refer to the chart above if you get lost trying to understand abbreviations in patterns and projects. Eventually, you will memorize them, but a chart is always helpful when you're just starting. For an added benefit, you'll find a symbols chart below.

symbols	US crochet term	British crochet term
●	slip stitch	
○	chain stitch	
X	single crochet	double crochet
+	single crochet	double crochet
T	half double crochet	half treble crochet
Ŧ	double crochet	treble crochet
X̃	crab stitch	
Ā	double crochet two together (dc2tog)	
V	2-hdc into same stitch	
V	2-dc into same stitch	
ⵔ	3-hdc cluster (bobble)	

Chapter 4

Getting Started

For the left-handed crafters out there, you are well aware of how confusing it can be to follow right-handed methods and adjust them to suit your needs. Crochet patterns and instructions are made for right-handers unless otherwise mentioned.

There are so few left-handed crafters and being a minority, there are not many sources available to learn from. This is because only a small percentage of people are left-handed and most of them are men. So, when it comes to doing crafts, particularly crafts for women, instructions for left-handers are not a priority.

Most left-handed women use right-handed instructional tools and prefer to use those. They end up learning how to crochet with their right hand. This may be alright for some whereas others don't have as much coordination in their right hand to create a smooth rhythm. It is also possible to follow right-handed instructions and adjust them accordingly so that you can use your left hand to crochet. This can work but it is confusing at times and one needs to concentrate carefully.

So, if you are a lefty and you intend to take up crochet as a hobby, this guide should be very useful and hopefully make the process a lot easier for you.

Let's Get Started

The most important thing is to get a firm and comfortable grip on your crochet hook as this will allow you to proceed to the next step. So, once you have a grip on it with your left hand, you'll need to use your right hand for holding the yarn. This is simply the opposite of what right-handers do.

You choose, as right-handers do, to hold your crochet hook using your thumb and your index finger to keep it in place, or you can simply grip it as you would a knife. Both ways are easy to get used to, so just decide which one you prefer using and learn to crochet that way.

There are, of course, several ways that you can hold your yarn as you work your stitches and that is up to you. One of the most commonly used methods is to loop the yarn using your right index finger. Keep the loose end up and then allow the thread that is attached to the yarn to lie on your palm in a cross manner. Once you have done this you can use the free end of the yarn to create a slip knot to start the crochet process.

Once you have done that, using your right hand then hold the slip knot you have made between your fingers' middle and thumb. This is the most comfortable position for this. Your yarn will be between your index finger and your thumb, so you' be able to control your tension nicely using your index finger. Controlling your tension will help you to create consistent, even stitches. It is best to master this from the beginning as it will make a huge difference to the quality of your work later on.

What Is the Difference Between Right and Left-Handed Crafters?

Although it is confusing to change hands when crocheting, the main differences between right-handed and left-handed techniques are as follows:

You either grip your crochet hook in your right or left hand.

You'll hold the yarn in your free hand.

The direction you work in changes as a left-hander as you'll work your stitches from left to right whereas a right-hander will do the opposite.

To work the stitches in rounds, left-handers will work in a counter-clockwise direction to the right. Right-handers will do the opposite and work their stitches in a clockwise direction to the left.

Crochet rounds worked by left-handers have a different appearance compared to those made by right-handers. Although some right-hand-ed crocheters think that left-handers' rounds look odd, others actually prefer them.

Rows worked by left-handers look the same as those done by right-handers, except that the yarn has been fastened off on the other end, so that is the only difference.

Once you start, you'll have a piece of yarn that hangs down; this is your yarn tail. Always leave the tail hanging and never crochet over it. If a pattern has a right side and a wrong side of the work, your tail can be used to give you a hint. When the tail is hanging on the bottom right-hand corner, and then that makes it the right side to work on.

Each time that you do the yarning over, you will pick up the yarn in a clockwise direction. This is a good point to remember at all times.

Working from Graphs

As a left-handed crafter, you'll find that most of the difficulties you'll have will lie in the interpretation of the patterns and graphs which you might use. Written patterns will be a challenge, whereas symbols are easier to use.

As an absolute beginner, you may not use graphs to start with. However, you are bound to come across them later on and use them. There are two different ones which you will use. The first is a graph used for color changes in your rows. These graphs make use of colored squares to represent the stitches. Hence, a red square indicates a red stitch in that row.

The second type of graph which you'll need to read is the graph used for the filet crochet technique (A). These are more complex and can be intimidating at first. The graph consists of blocks, which are filled in, and they represent three double crochet stitches which are worked into three separate stitches in the row above.

There are also open squares on the graph, and these are the mesh, consisting of double crochet and also chain stitches.

These graphs are marked with numbers representing the rows and stitches and are made for right-handed workers. Hence, as a left-hander, you'll need to just alter the graph accordingly. If you are not confident in doing so, you will still be able to use the graph as it is. However, the design will be reversed, and won't be exactly the same. This is not such a problem when it comes to basic designs and pictures but bear in mind that if there are any words on the graphs, they will appear as mirror images in the final product.

Here are some left-hander tips for reading graphs:

Left-handers should read the first row of the graph in the opposite direction, from left to right. Remember that right-hander will read it from right to left.

The stitches in filet graphs are normally different but the graphs read the same. For example: On the first row that falls on your right side is normally read from the left side onto right; this is the front side of the work done.

The first row of the right side gives you a basis of your work (front of work) will be read from left to right which means the work is okay while the wrong side (back of work) will be read from right to left.

Generally, the common patterns can be used by everyone, whether right or left-handed. Most of them will need to be changed slightly and also reversed. You'll learn how to do this by trial and error.

A basic adjustment that one might need to make is as follows: Join the yarn in the top left-hand corner of your piece. You'll need to do the opposite of course and join the yarn you are in use of to the upper right hand and to be specific the corner. Most times you will just need to reverse instructions such as these.

There is no need to avoid using a pattern because it is not made specifically for left-handers. The more you practice, the easier it becomes until eventually adjusting your patterns will become a habit.

A. Filet Crochet

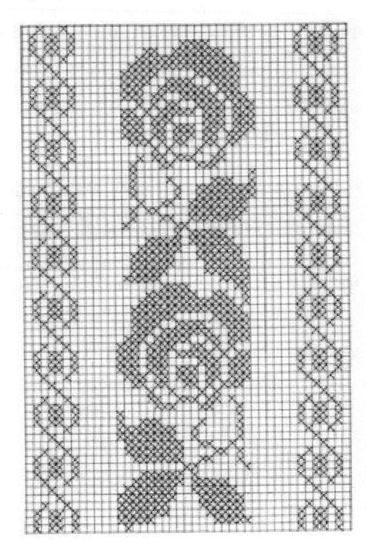

Chapter 5

Crochet Stitches

How to Yarn Over (YO)

We brought this in here because you can't do any crochet work without yarning over. In fact, you are going to yarn over and as much as possible during every crochet project. Yarn over gives you extra stitches on your crochet, and you can decide on how wide you want the holes on your piece when you yarn over.

Step 1: Create a slip knot – then you append in your hook in the knot (Instructions for slip knot available below)

Step 2: use the hand that you are using to hold the hook to also keep the tail of the slip knot to prevent it from getting wider or tighter.

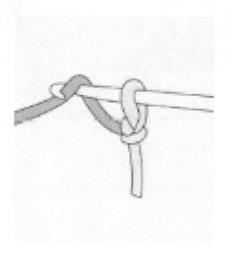

Step 3: Wrap the yarn from the back to the front (anticlockwise manner) of the hook (this is called a yarn over).

Step 4: take the yarn over the hook for the number of times instructed for the pattern.

1. How to Make a Slip Knot

You will start your crochet work with a slip knot, so you should be familiar with this. Do it over and over again till you master it.

Step 1: Measure about 7 inches to the end of the yarn.

Step 2: wrap it around your fingers to form a circle (a loop).

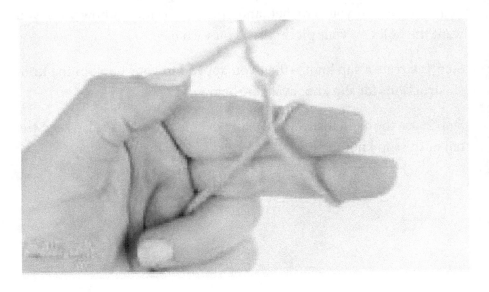

Step 3: Spread the loop formed with two of your fingers and put out the working yarn which is the longer strand into a loop with your fingers or a hook. Your loop should not be too tight.

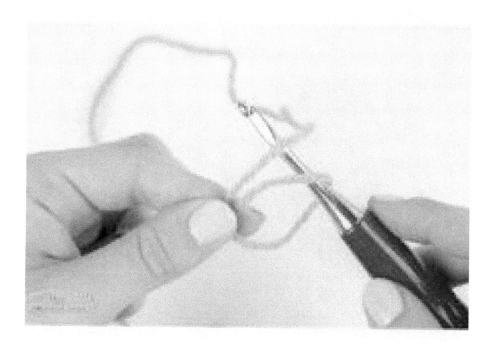

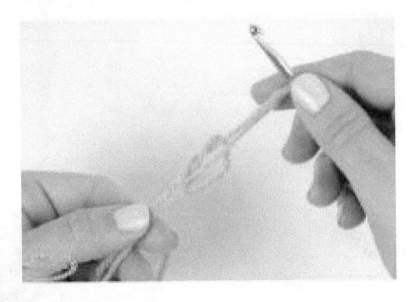

Step 4: Insert it on your hook.

2. How to make a Chain stitch (Ch.)

Many chain stitches, referred to as the base or foundation chain, make up the first row of a crochet piece.

Step 1: Create a slip knot – then you append in your hook in the knot.

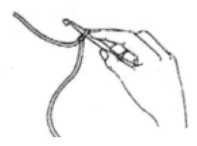

Step 2: Yarn over. After which you will then pull the yarn through the loop on the hook.

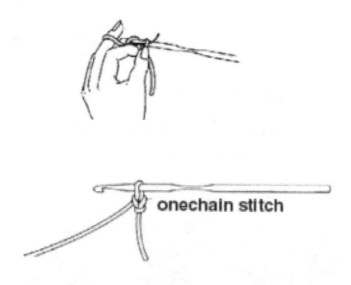

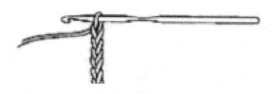

onechain stitch

Step 3: Ensure that you go through this process for as many chain stiches as required.

3. How to Single crochet (Sc)

In the UK, the Single crochet is usually referred to as double crochet. It is a fundamental stitch in crochet, and it provides a great way of joining crochet pieces. You can also use it as embroidery on a crochet piece.

Some crochet types basically use the single crochet as their primary stitch e.g., amigurumi.

Step 1: Make the base chain

Step 2: skip the first chain and insert your hook through the second chain.

Step 3: Yarn over (as explained above).

Step 4: pull the hook (thus pulling the yarn) through the loop. That is going to form two loops on the hook.

Step 5: Repeat the yarn over process while pulling the hook through the two loops to make a complete single crochet stitch.

This should leave you with just one look left on the hook. You can start your following stitch from this loop.

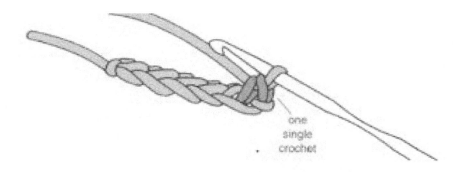

one
single
crochet

Depending on the required number of stiches for your project, you can create additional single crochet stitches to make up for them.

Moving to the following row while continuing the single crochet stitch:

Step 1: Without removing the crochet hook, turn your crochet piece from right to left (in an anticlockwise manner)

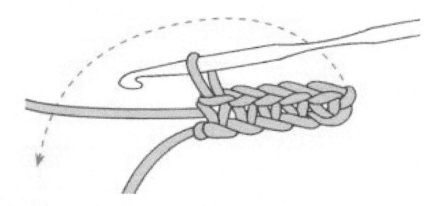

Step 2: Let the hook go into the last stitch of the first Sc row as illustrated below.

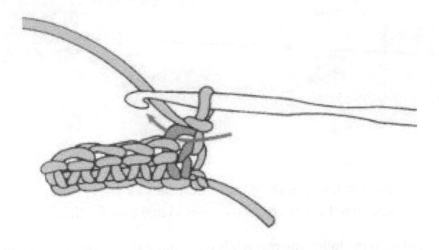

Step 3: Yarn over. Let the yarn pass through the last stitch to create two loops on the hook.

Step 4: Repeat the Yarn over again while ensuring that the yarn passes through both loops.

Ideally, you shouldn't have more than one loop left by now – that is you creating your first single crochet stitch.

How to decrease a single crochet stitch

The abbreviation for this is sc2tog.

To decrease a single crochet stitch is simply to join it to another to make both one.

Single crochet stitches that often come out in rectangular or square forms are transformed into clothing or other stuff this way.

To get your desired shape, reduce the number of stitches that exist on the row in which the two is being joined together.

The two stitches are joined at the top, which means that after decreasing, there will be two crochet bases sharing one top.

Step 1: Using one of the pieces, let your hook go into the following stitch where the reduction of the single crochet will begin (assuming the reduction should ideally to start at the beginning of the row, then, you should make use of your first stitch)

Step 2: Create two loops by yarning over and pulling up a loop.

Step 3: Leave these 2 loops you just created and then into the following stitch, of the second single crochet, insert your hook.

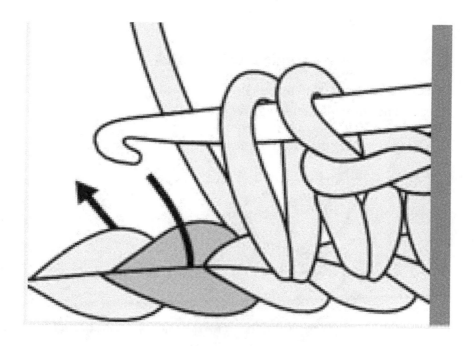

Step 4: Repeat the yarn over to create a 3rd loop.

Step 5: Do a last yarn over and pull through all the 3 loops you have created on the hook to close the stitch.

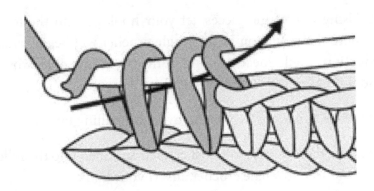

How to increase a single crochet stitch

This is easier than decreasing. You only need to work two single crochet stitches in the stitch wherever you are told to increase.

Working another stitch in the one indicated by the arrow

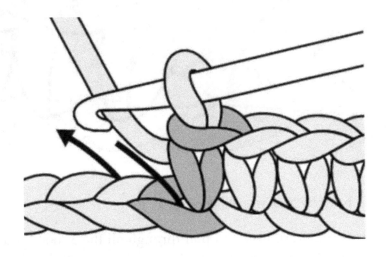

Will look like this:

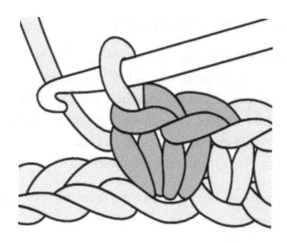

One stitch, different styles

You can try out different styles with the single crochet stitch such as:

1. A lacier style: To create this, instead of sliding the hook under the two loops, you want to insert your hook into the front loop only of the stitch (flo) - This will create more holes in your work.

2. A closed-up style: In a case where you do not want the holes, rather you want your work closed up; you can put your hook through the bottom left. Alternate between front loop only (flo) and back loop only (blo) to get your desired style.

3. A stretchy style: So, you fancy neither the open nor the "too close" style, but you would rather have your material to 'draw,' you might want to consider inserting the hook through the back loop only (blo).

4. A standard single crochet stitch style: you get this when you insert hook through the two loops of the stitch at the same time.

4. How to Make a Half Double Crochet (Hdc)?

UK will call this a half-treble crochet as against the half double crochet in US terms. This type of crochet is taller than a single crochet. It is lower than a double crochet. So, when you are trying to form your own patterns, and you need something that is midway between a single crochet and a double crochet, think of an Hdc. It can be worked at the edge of a scarf or blanket to add more beauty to the crochet piece.

Step 1: make your base chain stitch for the number of Hdc stitches required for the project

Step 2: Add another chain as extra.

Step 3: While ignoring the first 2 chains as they will service as turning chains, yarn over and insert hook from front to back in the center of the third chain.

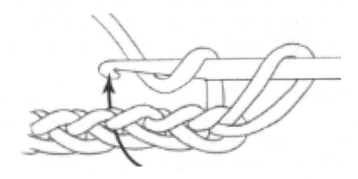

Step 4: Yarn over and draw the hook (by drawing the hook, you draw the yarn) through the chain to form three loops on the hook.

Step 5: Yarn over and draw yarn through all the three loops on the hook. There should be one loop on your hook now. That is the first half double crochet stitch.

To continue with Hdc on that row

Step 6: In the center of the following chain, yarn over and insert hook.

Step 7: Again, yarn over, but this time, pull the yarn through the loop to create 3 loops on the hook.

Step 8: Yarn over and pull the yarn through all the 3 loops you created to form the second half double crochet.

Step 9: Repeat steps 6-8 to continue working Hdc on that row.

Moving on to the following row

Step 10: Turn your work. Turning chain 2

Step 11: skip the first Hdc that is below the turning chain. Use the second one instead.

Step 12: Insert your hook from front to back and yarn over under the top two loops of the second Hdc.

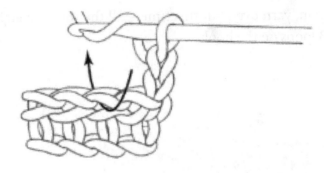

Step 13: While pulling the yarn through the stitch, yarn over just once.

Step 14: Repeat the yarn over process and pull the yarn through 3 loops on the hook to form the first half crochet stitch on that row.

Step 15: To continue working Hdc on that row, repeat steps 12-14

And just like a single crochet stitch, an instruction might call for the increase or decrease of a half double crochet. When it does, just do this:

Half double crochet increase (hdcinc):

When you increase in half double crochet, what you are simply doing is turning one stitch into two. The pattern instruction should tell you the particular stitch to work this into.

Step 1: Make double crochet stitch (instructions above)

Step 2: Create another Double crochet stitch in the very same stitch.

Half double crochet decrease (hdcdec):

Also, popularly referred to as half double crochet two together (hdc-2tog), you can make it with these steps:

Step 1: First, you should not that what you are trying to do is to create half double crochets into not less than 2 chains without actually completing them. And to this this, you need to yarn over and insert hook into the chain to be used. Repeat the yarn over again and then pull up a loop to make 3 loops on your hook.

Step 2: Create 5 loops by repeating Step 1 for the following chains.

Step 3: Lastly, YO and then make the yarn draw through all 5 loops – after which you will then have your half double crochet decrease.

5. How to Make a Double Crochet Stitch

Double crochet stitches are twice the length of single crochet stitches. Crocodile stitches are typical examples of stitches you use a double crochet stich for. It is also used to decorate the edges of some crochet works.

Step 1: make the base chain to the desired length.

Step 2: YO while fixing your hook at the end of the 3rd chain from the hook.

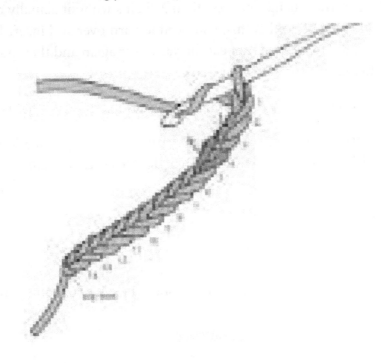

Note: The third chain is marked in red.

Step 3: Create 3 loops by YO while pulling the yarn through the third chain.

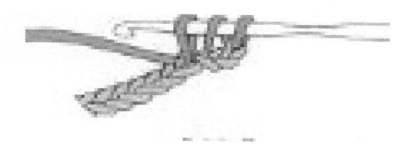

Step 4: Create 2 loops by YO while pulling the yarn through the first two loops.

Doing as instructed and shown above will give this:

Step 5: yarn over again and pull the yarn through the two loops to complete your first double crochet stitch.

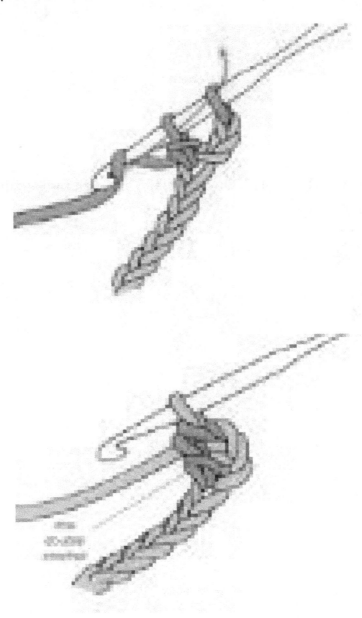

Step 6: to continue the double crochet on the following row, turn chain 3

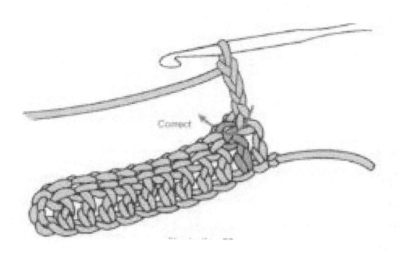

Chapter 6

Crochet Patterns: Beginners

DIY Scarves

Scarves are often rather straight forward when it comes to crochets, and you will find yourself making them rather quickly with the movements of that you have learned so that you do it efficiently and within a short time.

When you have finished with creating the foundation chain, you will then you will use the turning chai to create a long thin rectangle that you can keep knitting depending on how long and thus, how thick you want the scarf to be. As a beginner, this is a task that could take you a couple of hours a day, but you will be much satisfied with the outcome once you make it past the first couple of stitches.

Granny Square

This is a prevalent crochet pattern, and you will, therefore, find great value in knowing how to go through it.

You will begin by creating the slip knot and then creating three chains. Then you start using the double crochet so that you end up with double stitches. Then once you do this, loop the two double stitches through the third chain.

Then after this, create another three of such dc clusters so that, but now you will move the dc into the foundation of the first round.

When you finish with this, repeat the first two steps, then, repeat this process, beginning with a new foundation chain from the end of one dc stitch as you create the stitching until you get to the size of the granny square that you want.

You will then use the granny square on whatever you may want, from small table mats to covers for items in the house such as sound systems and TV sets. Depending on how you have woven it, you can also use it as a cover for pillows or small furniture like stools.

This is an example of a granny square. As we see, it alternates between Sc and dc, as well as loops on chains and rows.

Crochet Socks

Crochet socks are other easy designs that you will find it easier to so when you are a beginner.

According to Clara Parkes, the best yarns for socks are those that are elastic, meaning that they will need to stretch when you dip your foot into it, then wrap around the foot comfortably and warmly once you have worn it.

You will use your basic crochet techniques when you do this, while you will need additional experience to make more complex socks like ankle high socks and those with frilled edges or fancy patterns.

However, if you want simple, ankle-length socks, here you will need to alternate between the single crochet and double crochet. You will alternate between these two, lapping them over each other as you move through the foundations' chains, leaving the fabric closely-knit. This is what we call the seed stitch crochet.

So, you are being with your foundation chain and then flip it over and begin to work on the turning chain, and then make the first stitch, which will work as your first double crochet in the first row. Then, start to alternate between the dc and SC, once you make your first dc, then, make the Sc after that, then the dc, Sc as you progress. Then make these stitches across the rows. When you start with a dc, you will then end the row with sc.

Once you finish, turn it over and begin working on the turning chain. But since you will have flipped over the wool, you will be working in reverse, your dc going above Sc and your Sc going above dc.

To continue creating the rows that you need, repeat the process from the moment when you made your first dc. You will repeat this process depending on how long you want the socks to be, though as a beginner, you should probably make it as short as possible as you work on your hand movements and ironing out the problems that may arise when you make a mistake.

Crochet Seat Covers

You will find these in many homes and cars, providing the room with an antique, authentic, and comforting feel. And the thing about these is that the patterns are relatively easy to follow, with the size and design also mainly depending on how you want it. But you will want to keep it straight if you're going to create an extensive material.

Once you have done your slip knot and created your foundation chain, then make four stitches and two rows. Then, in the first round, create eight single crochet stitches then make two Sc stitches in each stitch.

In this, as with the socks, you will alternate between dc and sc. Once you create the two first rows, create another chain. Then, on the first row, the fourth chain from the hook, make dc through until the end of the row. Then, on the second chain, on the second row, make double crochet until then end. Repeat this on the third row, third chain. Once you have finished these, and then close the terms. At this point, you will have a square granny design, and you will then work from here through with additional rows and chains depending on how long you want it to be and how much you want it to cover the seat.

However, if you want to add on color and make it larger, create additional rows and chains using wool from the color that you want to infuse to the cover.

Square Blanket

This is one other straightforward pattern that you can learn. This one will also turn out great with just one color, though you will then have to put a lot of time into it so that you can achieve the thickness and size that you want.

Using the basis of the granny square, make your foundation chain then create three more. Begin to make double crochets then, and then loop them to create double stitches. After this, then connect these two double stitches through the third chain. After this, create another three dc but with the dc going into the foundation of the first round.

Go through this step until you get to the size that you desire. Or extra thickness, you could use the technique of socks and use alternating dc and Sc to create additional loops and knots to the width that you desire.

Alternatively, you can still use this basis to create table cover, but then you will not need to make it substantial and thick as you would have with a blanket.

Crochet Sweater for Beginners

The basis of making the sweater is starting from how you would make the granny square. Make two of such rectangles, with the size depending on who you are making it. Use dc for making the rectangle that you will make the front so that it is one solid piece with minimal gaps. You could also use this for the back or use Sc to leave a see-through back for extra aesthetics.

So, create nine chains, with two rows. Here, make an "Sc" through the second chain from the hook. Make a total of 8 sc. In the second row, stitch across the first chain, back loops only (blo). Then repeat this with the second row to row 65 or above, depending on the size to fit on waist, chest, and hips. Note that you will need the rows to be odd numbers.

Then move to the first row and in the first chain, turn it and make Sc across the band, with one running across each row, down to the number of rows that you have for the sweater and the region it fits. In the second row, loop through the third chain, turn and make double crochet across all rows. In the third row, repeat the second process. Through the fourth row through to the seventh, make the stitches on the chain lose.

Then in the 8th row, go through the third chain, turn it and make a double crochet in each dc and chain space so that you create a close-knit loop through each row until the end. In the 9th row, the third chain, make dc across all rows until the end. Use this technique for the back rectangle, but then you will use Sc and dc alternately depending on if you want the gaps or not.

Crochet with Plastic Rings

Pure fun brings crocheting with plastic rings. A brisk job that brings results quickly. However, you should not crochet the rings individually but create coherent chains.

Making a Crochet Ring

To start, put the normal crochet start loop on the plastic ring. The loop for the first solid ash and all subsequent hands is always pulled through the ring. Then, as usual, the two loops that are on the needle are embraced with an envelope. Repeat this until the ring is completely crocheted. Before you start work, crochet a ring completely to the sample to know how many units are needed overall. This is also dependent on wool strength.

Connect Rings Together

The connection between two rings takes place when the first plastic ring is crocheted in half with solid hands. Now, crochet an air mesh and then the first solid mesh around the following ring.

The last ring of a row is always completely crocheted. All other half-finished crocheted rings will be completed in the second round with solid hands. In doing so, always crochet a solid piece of ash around the connecting air mesh. In the end, pull the thread through the last stitch and sew it.

The second row of rings can now also be half crocheted and connected to the rings of the first row. When crocheting the first half of the second row of rings, add the already finished first row of rings. To do this, crochet a slit stitch into the middle stitch of the already finished ring row.

The crochet with plastic rings is particularly suitable for original placemats, small coasters, and the design of fabric bags, which receive such a special design. Of course, all these suggestions are also suitable for individual gifts.

Filethäkeln

This crochet resembles a knotted net. One can easily distinguish between an open and closed grid background. Below is the open grid background. This is intended to make it easier for you to start, as you will usually be crocheting according to a counting pattern that is attached to the instructions.

Crochet Flowers

These flowers are crocheted with wool for a crochet hook of strength 4 in rounds, and each of them is closed with a Kettmasche.

- Close the chain of 6 meshes with a chain stitch to the ring.

- 1st round: 12 fixed Sts.

- 2nd round: in every M. 2 tr. (Replace the first trump with 3 Ch.).

- 3rd round: Instead of the first tr. 3 Ch., Then into the first St. 1 tr., in the following M. Crochet 1 TR and 1 half TR

* At the following 4 m. in each puncture site 1 solid St., 1 half St. and 1 St., then 2 St., in the 4. Crochet 1 TR and 1 half TR. *

Repeat 4 times and replace the 6th sheet with 1 solid M., 1 complete half tr. and 1 tr. Cut the thread and pull it through. You can combine several individual motifs into one flower, or you can stitch together two individual motifs in different colors. Thus, simple blankets and crocheted with raffia, even carpets.

Chapter 7

Crochet Patterns: Intermediate

Gingerbread Man

Materials

- 4 Ply worsted weight yarn (shades of brown)

- Crochet hook

- Sequins or beads (to be used for the eyes, mouth and buttons)

- Glue

Directions

Head

1. Round 1: Chain 3, 11 half double crochets in 3rd chain from the hook. Join with a slip stitch in the top of ch-2. (You will now have 12 stitches)

2. Round 2: Chain 1, 2 single crochets in each stitch all the way round. Join with slip stitch in first single crochet and fasten off. Leave 6" of yarn for attaching to the body. (You will now have 24 stitches)

Body and arms

1. Row 1: Chain 9, single crochet in 2nd chain from hook, single crochet into each chain all the way across, turn. (You will have 8 stitches)

2. Rows 2 to 8: Chain 1, single crochet into each stitch, all the way across and turn. Do not turn or fasten off the yarn at the end of the last row.

3. Row 9: For first arm, working at the ends of the rows, chain 1, single crochet into each of the following 3 rows. Leave the remaining rows unworked and turn.

4. Rows 10 to 11: Chain 1. Single crochet into each stitches across and turns.

5. Row 12: Chain 1, skip first stitch, 3 single crochet into the following stitch

6. Row 9: For the second arm, work in the end of rows on the opposite side of the body. Join the brown yarn with a single

crochet in row 6, single crochet into each of the last 2 rows, turn. (You will have 3 stitches)

7. Rows 10 to 12: Repeat the same pattern as with that of the first arm. Sew the head to the top of the body between the arms.

Legs

1. Row 1: For first leg, with the wrong side of the body facing you, work on the opposite side of row 1. Join with a single crochet into the first stitch, single crochet into each of the following 3 stitches leaving the remaining stitches unworked, turn. (You will now have 4 stitches)

2. Rows 2 to 5: Chain 1, single crochet into each stitch across and turn.

3. Row 6: Chain 1, skip first stitch, single crochet into the following stitch, 2 single crochets into the following stitch, 3 single crochets into the last stitch, slip stitch into the end of row 5, fasten off.

4. Row 1: For second leg, with the right side of the body facing you work on the opposite side of Row 1. Join with a single crochet in the first stitch, single crochet into each of following 3 stitches, turn. (You will now have 4 stitches)

5. Rows 2 to 6: Repeat the same pattern as with that of the first leg.

Finishing

1. Edging for the Gingerbread Man: Using the left-over yarn from the head, join with a single crochet the first row of the arm near the head. Single crochet into each stitch, all the way round. At

the end of each row work with a slip stitch as you go around to the following stitch and join with a slip stitch into the first single crochet. Fasten off the yarn.

2. Around the outer edge of the Gingerbread Man, glue a piece of rickrack, or sew a chain stitch in a different color all the way round the edges.

3. Glue two blue beads or sequins 1/8" apart for the eyes over top of round 1 on the head. Glue three red beads or sequins over bottom of round 1 on the head for the mouth. Glue three green beads or sequins to the front of the body as buttons.

Crochet Holiday Pinecones

Materials

- Cotton yarn

- Crochet hook 5.5 mm

- Tapestry needle

Directions

1. Start off the pines by making a magic loop. The pinecones will be made in rounds. Round 1: 6 single crochets into the ring and pull closed. Round 2: Make 2 single crochet in each single crochet all the way round (You will now have 12 single crochets). Round 3: * single crochet into the following single crochet * repeat from * all the way round (You will now have 18 single crochets).

2. Round 4: * single crochet into the following two single crochet, increase into the following * repeat pattern * all the way round (You will now have 24 single crochets). Round 5: * single crochet into the following three single crochet, increase into the following * repeat pattern * all the way round (You will now have 30 single crochets).

3. Round 6 a: In the front loops only, *slip stitch and chain 3 into one stitch, double crochet into following, slip stitch into the following - 3 stitches* repeat pattern * all the way round, chain 1 (You will now have 10 "petals" plus chain 1). Round 6 b: In the back loops of round 5, *single crochet into the following 8, decrease once* repeat pattern * all the way round, join, chain 1 (You will now have 27 single crochets). Round 7: Single crochet into each single crochet all the way round (You will have 27 single crochets).

4. Round 8 a: In the front loops only, *slip stitch and chain 3 into one stitch, double crochet into the following, slip stitch into the following - 3 stitches* repeat pattern * all the way round, chain 1 (You will now have 9 "petals" plus chain 1). Round 8 b: In the back loops of round 7, *single crochet into the following 7, decrease once* repeat the pattern * all the way round, join, chain 1

(You will now have 24 single crochets). Round 9: Single crochet into each single crochet all the way round (You will now have 24 single crochets).

5. Round 10 a: In the front loops only, *slip stitch and chain 3 in one stitch, double crochet into following, slip stitch into following - 3 stitches* repeat the pattern * all the way round, chain 1 (You will now have 8 "petals" plus chain 1). Round 10 b: In the back loops of round 9, *single crochet into the following 6, decrease once* repeat the pattern * all the way round, join, chain 1 (You will now have 21 single crochets). Round 11: Single crochet in each single crochet all the way round (You will now have 21 single crochets).

6. Round 12 a: In the front loops only, *slip stitch and chain 3 in one stitch, double crochet into the following, slip stitch into the following - 3 stitches* repeat the pattern * all the way round, chain 1 (You will now have 7 "petals" plus chain 1). Round 12 b: In the back loops of round 11, *single crochet into the following 5, decrease once* repeat the pattern * all the way round, join, chain 1 (You will now have 18 single crochets). Round 13: Single crochet into each single crochet all the way round (You will now have 18 single crochet).

7. Round 14 a: In the front loops only, *slip stitch and chain 3 in one stitch, double crochet into the following, slip stitch into the following - 3 stitches* repeat pattern * all the way round, chain 1 (You will now have 6 "petals" plus chain 1). Round 14 b: In the back loops of round 13, *single crochet into the following 4, decrease once* repeat the pattern * the entire round, join, chain 1 (You will now have 15 single crochets). Round 15: Single crochet into each single crochet all the way round (You will now have 15 single crochets).

8. Round 16 a: In the front loops only, *slip stitch and chain 3 in one stitch, double crochet into the following, slip stitch into the following - 3 stitches* repeat pattern * all the way round, chain 1 (You will now have 5 "petals" plus chain 1). Round 16 b: In the back loops of round 15, *single crochet into the following 3, decrease once* repeat the pattern * all the way round, join, chain 1 (You will now have 12 single crochets). Round 17: Single crochet into each single crochet all the way round (You will now have 12 single crochets).

9. Round 18 a: In the front loops only, *slip stitch and chain 3 in one stitch, double crochet into the following, slip stitch into the following - 3 stitches* repeat pattern * all the way round, chain 1 (You will now have 4 "petals" plus chain 1). Round 18 b: In the back loops of round 17, *single crochet into the following 2, decrease once* repeat the pattern * all the way round, join, chain 1 (You will now have 9 single crochets). Round 19: Single crochet into each single crochet all the way round (You will now have 9 single crochets). Round 20: In the front loops only, *slip stitch and chain 3 into one stitch, double crochet into the following, slip stitch into the following - 3 stitches* repeat the pattern * all the way round (You will now have 3 "petals"). Fasten off the yarn and thread through the loose ends.

Chapter 8

Crochet Patterns: Advanced

Triangle

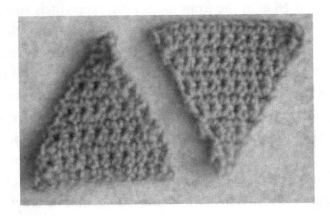

Materials: Choose any yarn color and hook size comfortable for you as this is a very simple project.

Gauge: Use any gauge for this project.

Make 14 chain stitches.

Round 1: Single crochet in the first chain stitch from the hook and each chain stitch across. You will make a total of 13 single crochets.

Round 2: Single crochet two stitches together. Make one single crochet in each of the following 9 stitches. Single crochet two stitches together.

Make 1 chain stitch then turn.

Round 3: Do one single crochet in each stitch across the row. You will have a total of 11 single crochet stitches in the row.

Make 1 chain stitch then turn.

Round 4: Single crochet two stitches together. Make one single crochet in each of the following seven stitches Single crochet two stitches together

Make 1 chain stitch then turn.

Round 5: Make one single crochet on each stitch across the row. You'll have a total of nine single crochet stitches in the row.

Make 1 chain stitch then turn.

Round 6: Single crochet two stitches together. Make one single crochet in each of the following five stitches. Single crochet two stitches together.

Make 1 chain stitch then turn.

Round 7: Do a single crochet in each stitch across the row. You'll have a total of seven single crochet stitches in the row.

Make 1 chain stitch then turn.

Round 8: Repeat Round 7.

Round 9: Single crochet two stitches together. Make one single crochet in each of the following three stitches. Single crochet two stitches together.

Make 1 chain stitch then turn.

Round 10: Make one single crochet in each stitch across the row. You'll have a total of five single crochet stitches in the row.

Make 1 chain stitch then turn.

Round 11: Single crochet two stitches together. Make one single crochet in the following stitch Single crochet two stitches together.

Make 1 chain stitch then turn.

Round 12: Make one single crochet in each stitch across the row for a total of three single crochet stitches in the row.

Make 1 chain stitch then turn.

Round 13: Single crochet two stitches together.

Round 14: Make one chain stitch. Work a round of slip stitch all the way around the outer edge of the triangle shape, putting one extra chain stitch in corners if desired, including the one at the top of the triangle. The extra chain stitch makes the corners a bit pointier.

Weave in loose ends and break the yarn.

Round

Materials:

- Your choice of yarn

- Crochet hook size H-8

Gauge: Use any gauge for this project.

To make flat round crochet designs, you need to begin by making two chain stitches.

Important note per round: For each new round, add one extra single crochet stitch to the number of single crochet stitches between increases (increase is done by making two single crochets in one stitch).

Round 1. Make six single crochets in the second chain stitch from the hook. Slip stitch in the first single crochet to join.

Round 2: Make one chain stitch and two single crochets in each single crochet around. Slip stitch in the first single crochet to join – making twelve single crochets.

Round 3: Do one chain stitch. Join the single crochet in the following single crochet, two single crochets in the following single crochet. Repeat this around. Slip stitch in the first single crochet to join – making eighteen single crochets.

Round 4: Make a chain stitch. Do a single crochet in each of the following two single crochets, and two single crochets in the following single crochet. Repeat this around. Slip stitch in the first single crochet to join – making twenty-four single crochets.

Spiral Flower

Materials:

- Your choice of yarn

- Crochet hook size G-6

Gauge: Use any gauge for this project.

Feel free to choose any yarn color to make this very stylish design!

To make the foundation, follow these rounds:

Round 1: Make four chain stitches. Join it with a slip stitch to the first chain to form a ring.

Round 2: Do eleven chain stitches. Slip stitch in the second chain from the hook and do this for the remaining nine chains. Slip stitch into the center of the ring. Turn your work 180 degrees clockwise but do not flip. Slip stitches the center of the ring.

Round 3: Work in back loops only. Single crochet into the first stitch, then make a half double crochet on the second stitch. Half double crochet into the third stitch, double crochet into the fourth stitch, double crochet into the fifth stitch. Do a turning chain into the sixth stitch; make another two on the seventh stitch, and another on the eight. Double turn chain into the ninth stitch then another on the tenth

Round 4: Make two chain stitches and turn your work.

Round 5: Work in back loops only. Slip stitch into each of the following twelve stitches. Slip stitch again into the center of the ring.

To make the petals, follow these rounds:

Round 1: Make a chain stitch and turn your work.

Round 2: Work on the front loops of the foundation, single crochet into the first stitch. Half double crochet into the second stitch. Do the same for the third. Make two double crochets into the fourth stitch. Double crochet into the fifth stitch and make a turning chain into the sixth stitch. Make two turning chains into the seventh stitch, and one of the eight. Now, do a double turn chain into the ninth and tenth stitch. After this, you should have two stitches remaining.

Round 3: Make two chain stitches and turn your work.

Round 4: Work in back loops. Slip stitch into each of the following twelve stitches. Slips stitch the center of the ring.

Round 5: Repeat Round 1-4 until you make 10 petals.

Weave in your ends.

Octagon

Materials:

- Your choice of yarn color

- Crochet hook size H-8

Gauge: Use a 5-inch gauge for this project.

Have a stylish octagon shaped center piece for your living room! Just choose the yarn color that you like and follow these easy steps.

Round 1: Make five chain stitches and slip stitch into the beginning chain to form a circle. Make three double crochets. Do fifteen double crochets on the ring. Join into the top of first double crochet with slip stitch. You should have sixteen double crochets.

Round 2: Do two double crochets in the same stitch as the chain three earlier. Make a double crochet in the following double. Make three double crochets in the following double. Make a double crochet in the following double. Repeat this until you get to the beginning of the chain.

Now, slip stitch in the top of the beginning chain. You should have thirty-two double crochets.

Round 3: Now, chain stitch three times for round three. Make three double crochets in the following double crochet, make one double crochet in the following three double crochets. Repeat until end. Make three double crochets in the following double crochet. Do one double crochet in following two. Join with slip stitch at the top of the first double crochet. Now, you should have forty-eight double crochets.

Round 4: Make three chain stitches for round four. Make a double crochet in the following double crochet. Make three double crochets in the following double crochet. Make one double crochet in the following five double. Repeat until end. Make three double crochets in the following double crochet. Make on double crochet in the following three. Join all with a slip stitch at the top beginning of the chain.

Round 5: Fasten end, cut yarn and weave using an octagon tapestry needle. Last round should make sixty-four double crochets.

Chapter 9

———— ❧ ————

Simple Amigurumi Project

What is Amigurumi crochet?

This type of crochet is said to have originated from Japan. People would use this type of crochet when making toys that would be stuffed using this crochet. Ami means knitting or yarn that has been crocheted while amigurumi means a doll that has been stuffed. This type of crochet is therefore used when one is making these stuffed dolls through the use of heavy yarn. One can also make fan items and the large novelty cushions as well as the homewares.

Heart Amigurumi Pattern

I've chosen a pattern that is pretty basic when it comes to amigurumi. There aren't any intricate details, whatsoever, so this project is perfect for absolute beginners. For this pattern, you can use a 2 mm crochet hook, but you may also try with a slightly bigger hook and see what looks better.

To start off, you will make a magic ring and work six single crochet (Sc) into the magic ring. Now, if you don't know how to make a magic ring, it is pretty simple.

All you need to do is to make a loop and almost as if you are making a chain pull the yarn to the front and chain one, then stitch Sc around the ring, preferably six or seven Sc and pull the yarn tail to tighten.

All you need to do is secure with a slip stitch and your first round is complete. You also need to weave in the end so that it doesn't unravel.

The reason why amigurumi start with a magic ring is that it doesn't leave a big hole in the center, unlike chaining and creating a ring out of chains. This way, you can tighten the ring as much as you would like. For the second round, you will do six increases by working two Sc into each of the Sc from the last round.

For the third round, you will work one Sc and an increase in the following. You will repeat these six times, which will result in 18 stitches at the end of the round. In the fourth round, you will crochet Sc in a Sc stitch and another in the following and then you will work an increase in the third stitch. You will repeat these six times, which will result in 24 stitches at the end of this round. In the fifth round, you will crochet seven Sc and then an increase, and repeat it two more times.

At the end of this round, you will have 27 stitches, and then for the following three rounds, Sc all the stitches. At the end of the ninth round, you will have 27 stitches. Fasten off the yarn and repeat this whole process for the second 'hump'. Once you have finished the second 'hump', do not fasten off, but join the two together. You will do this by slip stitching three of the stitches from both of the humps. This way, each of the humps will have 24 available stitches and three connected.

For the second part, you will create a wide part of the heart. You will Sc the tenth and eleventh round (48 stitches in total). Then you will begin decreasing. All the patterns will be repeated three times. For the following round, you will work 14 Sc and then one decrease.

Repeat these two more times (45 stitches in total). In the following round, you will work 13 Sc and then one decrease and again repeat these two more times (42 stitches). As you can see, a pattern arises. For each of the following rounds, you will crochet a certain number of stitches and then make a decrease and then repeat it two more times.

Each time you will decrease the number of stitches for three. It is that simple. At the end you will have six stitches. This is when you're going to insert the stuffing into your heart amigurumi and finish off the project. If you feel that it is finishing abruptly, then make another round of Sc once and decrease once, which will leave you with three stitches that can be worked together and then you can fasten off the yarn.

Emoji Amigurumi Pattern

The following pattern is also one of the easier and simpler in terms of crocheting the basis. However, it has some finishing details that may be a bit more complicated for some people; but all in all, I think it is still one of the easiest amigurumi patterns to make.

Again, I suggest using a smaller gauge hook, but if you feel like experimenting, please do so and if you are satisfied with the outcome, keep it that way. Essentially, you will be making an amigurumi ball that by adding different finishing details will turn into emoji.

Now, let's get started! To start off, make a magic ring and work six Sc into the ring. It would be a good idea to mark the beginning of the round with a different color yarn or a stitch marker, just so that you know whether you have finished around. In the second round, you will increase in all of the stitches. In the third round, you will work one Sc and increase once, and repeat these five more times.

This way, you will increase by six stitches, 18 in total. For the fourth round, crochet two Sc and increase once, and repeat these five more times. In the fifth round, you will crochet three Sc and increase once and repeat these five more times. For the final increase, you will cro- chet four Sc and increase once and repeat these five more times. If you want your ball to be bigger, you can continue this way until you reach the desired size. However, we will stop increasing here and Sc all the stitches without increasing for the rounds 7-12.

Once we have done the Sc for five rounds, we will start decreasing. We will do this by reversing what we lastly did.

Now, for the 13th round, you will crochet four Sc and decrease once and repeat these five more times. In the 14th round, crochet three Sc and decrease once and repeat until the end of the round. In the 15th round, crochet two Sc and decrease once; repeat five more times. In the 16th round, crochet one Sc and decrease once.

For the final round, you will work six decreases, and finish off. But, before that, you will fill the ball with stuffing and then work the final round. Crochet all of the remained stitches together and fas- ten off the yarn. Of course, if you want, you can make the ball in multiple colors.

Now that you have finished the base, which is the ball, you can work on the details. For eyes, you can crochet simple round motifs. For wide-open mouth, you can crochet a semicircle, either in rows or rounds. Sew them onto the ball and embroider the black details onto the ball. You can do this either with an embroidery needle or with a crochet hook. Though if you decide to try with a crochet hook, you may find it a bit difficult and the lines will be thicker. All in all, it is a fun little project and I'm sure that you definitely need one of these. If not for your children, then it is perfect for you. I would use it as an anti-stress ball, wouldn't you?

Chapter 10

Tips and Tricks

When you're new to something, everything might seem a tad overwhelming. Even if crocheting isn't a difficult hobby per se, this doesn't mean that it doesn't come with several challenges, especially during your first tryouts. Don't get discouraged, though, since we've all been there. What matters most is to keep going and you'll realize that you're steadily making progress.

Turn Skeins into Balls of Yarn before Starting Your Project

For one thing, you might feel impatient to get started with your very first crochet project. This might tempt you to rip the label off the skein of yarn and get started right away to see how things go. Nonetheless, even if you could crochet by using skeins of yarns, you might accomplish better results if you consider winding the skein into a ball first. As an expert, you won't tell the difference, but as a beginner, you will certainly see it.

If we were to compare balls of yarns with skeins, you should know they have several advantages. For one thing, they could help you avoid tangles. Usually, center-pull-skeins of yarn are prone to get tangled easily towards the end. On the other hand, balls of yarns don't tangle as much, which can really make the world of a difference if you want to simplify your work.

In addition to that, if you find it difficult to accomplish to right tension when crocheting, you should work from a ball of yarn as opposed to working from a ball of skein. To simplify this task, you could use ball winders – but you might also do it by hand.

Make Sure You Position the Yarn Correctly

It's always best to position the yarn correctly so that your project goes on smoothly. Basically, the ball of yarn should be positioned in such a way as to unwind easily as you crochet. Considering that you're crocheting at home from a comfortable chair, it might be a good idea to keep the ball on the floor by your feet or in your lap – depending on whichever option you prefer best.

On the other hand, if you're crocheting in a moving vehicle or in a plane, or any other place where you don't have a lot of space at your disposal, you should keep the ball inside a tote bag. This will prevent it from unwinding or rolling around.

When Needed, Change the Size of the Hook

Novice crochets have the tendency to stick to the hook they get started with. This must do, of course, with convenience and comfort. Many times, the type of hook you start to crochet with gives you a certain degree of assurance, which is why the temptation to keep using it is high. This is common not only for crochet but for other types of handwork as well, such as knitting, embroidery and the list could go on.

However, make sure you always consider the way in which your work evolves and make the necessary adjustments as you go. If you feel that your work seems too tight, you should simply switch the hook with a larger one. On the other hand, if you notice that the work appears a bit too loose, what you must do is choose a smaller crochet hook. Essentially, the hook size written on the yarn ball is merely a suggestion and you shouldn't follow it blindly.

As a rule of thumb, before starting a project – especially a complex one – it's best to give yourself time to do some experimenting.

Nevertheless, note that changing hooks in the middle of a project is contraindicated. That's because this will make your work appear inconsistent and uneven. And you don't want that. Even if you were to use the same size hooks from different manufacturers, you would still monitor several changes when you have a closer look at your project.

At the same time, depending on the type of hook you're using, this will impact the way in which you hold it and the way in which the stitching will look in the end.

Working on Your Tension: Why Is It So Important?

Working on your tension is important if you want to enhance your crocheting technique. In order to do this, you must keep the crochet in a way that feels comfortable – otherwise, enhancing your tension will be much more difficult. As we already pointed out, you should keep the crochet hook in the dominant hand – this depends whether you are right-handed or left-handed.

Rest assured, as a beginner to crocheting, you are bound to hold the hook either too tightly or too loosely. And while practice will most likely contribute to solving these issues, there are also some ways in which you can do that, and we'll outline them in the following paragraphs.

Pull from the center of the yarn

This could be very helpful when you feel that your tension is too loose or too tight. For example, when you pull the strand from the outside, this will make the skein bounce all over the place, which will most likely be an impediment in attaining the right level of tension. On the other hand, if you focus your attention on pulling the strand right from the center, it will glide through your fingers more easily – which will allow you to feel better about your tension.

Have a look at the way in which experts hold the hook

Although copying the technique of an expert might not be the safest solution to this tension problem, it could help. Most likely, you can have a look at numerous tutorials online and see the way in which other people use their hooks. Once you do that, you can try it yourself and see what works best for you. Remember, there are no good or wrong ways to do this. The good thing is that there are many free online resources that could get you started when you feel clueless.

Since each person works differently, if you realize that what you're looking at is not your style, you should simply look at another technique until you find someone that works in a similar way as you do.

Choose a beginner-friendly yarn

This is another useful tip if you feel that you're not making any progress. In fact, choosing a yarn that is difficult to work with might be an impediment, preventing you from making progress at a fast rate. On a different note, the tension you have when working with yarn will depend on the type of material you have chosen as well. For instance, as a beginner, your tension might be unsuitable if you're trying to work with cotton yarn, which poses some challenges to start with.

That isn't to say that all beginners will encounter difficulties when trying to work with cotton yarn, but some might. This is a subjective matter and you shouldn't feel bad or anything – it's just that when it comes to crafts, every person has his/her own rhythm of learning and progressing. This means you shouldn't put too much pressure on yourself if things are moving a bit slower than you anticipated they would.

As a rule of thumb, when you're still trying to figure out how to attain the perfect level of tension, it's best to choose a material that has a bit of stretch to it. This will make your job easier. Over time, you can diversify the types of materials you're working with, to ensure that you foster your skill and your creativity. But take your time.

In addition to that, we advise you to steer clear of novelty yarns or variegated yarns – particularly at the beginning of your crochet journey. These two types of yarns will make it especially hard to remain consistent in your stitches. Concurrently, these materials make it difficult to count the stitches, something that might be frustrating to beginners.

How to Avoid the Most Common Crochet Rookie Mistakes

Now that we've introduced some helpful tips on how to get better at crocheting, let's focus a bit on the most common mistakes you are bound to make as a rookie. Knowing these in advance can be beneficial, in the sense that you might avoid making them altogether, which will allow you to save time!

Crocheting in the front loop only

Novices to crocheting are bound to make this mistake. Therefore, we couldn't stress enough the importance of learning how to place the hook inside the stitch, as this represents the foundation of this handicraft. This mistake is likely to happen especially if the hook tends to slip from time to time and you don't realize this right away.

How do you avoid this common mistake? What you must do is simply have a closer look at the detailing of each row as you work. Basically, you should analyze each row. While this may seem tedious and time-consuming, if you practice enough, you'll get the hang of it and you won't have to do it any longer. In time, your stitches will become second nature to you, so you won't have to stress about it.

Your work seems to be getting wider and wider

This is likely to happen to anyone – beginners and advanced crocheting fans as well. Therefore, you shouldn't feel too discouraged if it seems to happen to you. This is bound to occur when you're not paying close attention to the stitches. On that note, one way to avoid this from happening is by counting your stitches – in this way, you will prevent ending up with more stitches than you had in mind when you first started working on this project.

You might be doubling up into one stitch or, without your willing, you might end up working a stitch in a turning chain. The safest and simplest way to prevent this from happening repeatedly is by counting your stitches. To that end, you might count each row as you finish, or keep an eye on the shape of your project and determine whether it is developing as you had in mind.

You might feel that this is time-consuming, but believe us; it is more time-consuming to realize that you've been working for hours in a row to realize that you've made a mistake and you have to do the entire thing all over again.

Not focusing on counting the rows while working

This mistake also has to do with maximizing your time. The same way in which it is advisable to count the stitches to the project you're doing; you should also count the rows to avoid unwanted mistakes. When you're crocheting, you can easily get distracted, as your mind tends to wander off, especially if you're watching a TV series or anything of the kind.

Staying focused is essential if you're just starting out, so make sure you are there, in the present, when working on your project. Otherwise, you'll realize that there are five extra rows of crochet and you have lost your valuable time. You might resort to utilizing a row counter in case you end up doing the same mistake repeatedly, as it will come in handy.

Chapter 11

⚜

Frequently Asked Questions

Here is a quick roundup of the most common questions that are asked about how to best care for your yarn or wool.

Can you wash an entire skein?

In some cases, you may need to wash the skeins or yarn balls before use (spillages etc.) and although this can be difficult it is possible. The trickiest part about this is to ensure that the yarn doesn't unravel which you can do by putting it in a pair of tights or washing bag beforehand. However, make sure to follow the same washing guidelines and check to see that all detergent has been rinsed out (you may need to hand rinse them to make sure as this could cause irritation if there is residue)

How often should you wash yarn or wool?

This depends on the amount of wear and the purpose of the project. For example, a crochet bag may only need to be sponged down once in a while whereas clothes would need to be washed more frequently. Clothes such as socks would definitely need to be washed after each use to avoid any fungal or bacterial infections while a jumper may be worn a few times before needing to be washed. It entirely depends.

Can you dye your own yarn?

The answer to this is yes and the easiest types of yarn to dye are those that are animal fibers, for example alpaca, wool or mohair. Make sure to protect your skin and clothes when dying your own yarn as it easily transfers and can cause a large mess. For synthetic yarn you will need to buy specific dye to use for the fiber.

How do you find yarn care instructions for other yarn?

Usually, yarn will come with a wraparound label that has specific washing instructions on the outside or overleaf of the label. Some special types of yarn will come with packet instructions and others may not come with anything at all. The more specialized the yarn is, the more likely you are to get instructions. Generally speaking, worsted weight yarn which is most commonly used is also more durable which means you are less likely to get specific instructions.

Can you get rid of old stains and smells?

Yes, however not always and a lot of dried on stains or lingering smells are hard to get rid of. The longer the stain or smell has been present on the fiber, the harder it is to get rid of.

Can you tumble dry?

It is best not to tumble dry yarn or wool as it is very sensitive to temperature and it can make it rough or coarse on the skin (as well as risk of shrinking) if it is exposed to higher temperatures. If you choose to use the tumble dryer it is best to do so on a cool or very low heat setting for short amounts at a time to check it is not having adverse effects on the fibers.

How long can you keep yarn or wool for?

Wool or yarn can be kept for a very long time over a range of years if it is stored properly in the right conditions and maintained. Wool that has been kept for over 10 years may not be viable for crocheting or knitting because it has started to degrade but this depends on the type.

Organic fibers that haven't been treated may not last as long as store-bought that have been chemically treated.

How do you store yarn?

Store In skeins or balls in a dry place and make sure to clean out and check frequently to avoid your stash coming into contact with a lot of dust, moths or pests that might contaminate the supply. In addition, avoid getting your stash wet and ensure that you frequently air it out to avoid there being a musty smell embedded in the yarn.

How to Read Crochet Patterns?

To my opinion, reading a pattern of crochet is important for learning simple crochet. You are very limited when it comes to finished projects unless you can read crochet patterns!

If you can't read a pattern for a crochet, I think you are very tight. What are you doing, keep going until you think it is right and start like that?

You have the world at your fingertips if you can read a crochet pattern. You're not afraid to try new stuff in my opinion!

However, I am fascinated by the number of people who cannot understand crochet patterns. It seems like a real shame that they don't know how to get better and feel better about their efforts!

If you cannot read a pattern of crochet, how do you make home-made dishcloths or crochets? Remember; in the picture they look fast, but can you double that?

When I started to crochet (it seems to have been a lifetime), these patterns with such unusual abbreviations were a challenge for me. At this point, I decided to learn how to read the patterns regardless.

I have done a lot of work and answered a variety of questions and have eventually obtained results. The odd thing was that even I wasn't even crocheting wool alone.

To be able to read crochet patterns would seem to encourage you to go higher–that's how I switched to cotton and made doilies in a very short time learning how to read patterns from crochet.

What scares me is that people who can't read crochet patterns don't seem to be careful to clarify and/or illustrate any of the crochet stitches on a one-on - one basis. This disturbs me.

I was told that it demonstrated a lack of maturity in someone who did crochet home in that way not to be able to read crochet patterns. It did not have any ambition!

Now I'm not in agreement, but I've got one I can tell–"Don't learn something at the half, learn the whole thing, or waste my time!" I could crochet a doily while my oldest daughter was in the hospital at the age of five (5) months, by reading crochet instructions.

Here is another thing to consider:

How do you increase your own crocheting skills to include extra stitches if you can't read crochet instructions or patterns? I mean the triple stitch, the half double stitch and so on–it could be overwhelming!

And if you're a home crocheter, learn how to read the patterns that I call never-ending, extend your scope beyond your standards.

Conclusion

Thank you for making it to the end. Finishing what you have woven is an achievement. The following step is to work your way through the techniques, so you can improve your skills in crocheting.

But before you get started on your projects, remember that it is important not to cut the strand flush with the knot after sewing. Because of repetitive use and washing, the cut knot would end up falling apart and could ruin what you have woven. For this, it is necessary that you leave enough thread to hide it and finish off the project well.

This also occurs with all strands derived from the junctions of clews and others. This type of thread trim will serve you both if you have knitted with the reverse of a jersey stitch. That said you also have to know that there is a multitude of different methods to join strands of clews. Here is a basic way of joining two clews:

1. Join on the edge of the work.

2. With the strand of the new skein, make a simple knot by wrapping the strand of the used skein. When you are knitting, there are times when you finish a ball, and you have to join with the beginning of another ball to continue knitting. The first thing you have to know is that never are two balls joined in the middle of knitted work. It is necessary to unite in the borders, that

is to say, at the beginning or at the end of a turn (although it seems to you that you are wasting wool).

3. Adjust that knot bringing it as close as possible to the needle (the new skein is now attached)

4. Make a knot between the strand of the skein used and the strand of the new skein (now the strand used is attached).

5. Start knitting with the new strand.

We hope you have at least learned the basics of crocheting. With some practice, hard work and dedication, you will master crocheting. There is no talent required for crocheting; it is just the passion and interest that will make you the expert in crocheting. There are even young children and adults who are now crocheting. It is all about practice. Some mistakes and failures will come your way while crocheting. But you should not get discouraged by it. All you need is continuously practicing, and with time you will master the art.

Crochet beginners and experts alike enjoy creating projects from patterns. Although it is possible to use the beginner stitches and make a blanket without a pattern, a pattern will provide more detail. Some patterns use small crochet appliques or alternating patterns and the project patterns show how to do it.

Many crocheters learn to make their own patterns and graphs from the abbreviations and symbols they have learned. Once you master all of the stitches you will be able to make your own patterns so others can make project you have designed.

Using patterns may seem difficult and overwhelming at first but once you are used to seeing the abbreviations and symbols your skills will improve. Stick to patterns and graphs for beginners, these use beginner stitches, so you can learn at your own pace.

Learning the skill to read and follow graphs and patterns will allow you to create more than just a scarf or simple throw. You will be able to complete heirloom quality projects, winter clothing such as sweaters, mittens, gloves, hats and scarfs, dresses, home décor such as doilies or place mats and runners, and even toys for the kids.

Use your new-found ability to make gifts for loved ones and friends alike. Everyone enjoys receiving a handmade item that is useful and beautiful. No matter what you decide to make, the time and effort you put into the creation will show in the finished product.

So, as you can see from this guide, crocheting is a skill that is easy to pick up, and fun to master. Once you have gotten to grips with each stitch and technique, working out patterns will quickly become natural and then you can create whatever you want, including your very own patterns.

Crocheting is a brilliant way to create unique, homemade gifts, with a personal touch, or even cute little additions to spice up your own home or wardrobe. There isn't a better feeling than creating something yourself, and seeing others admire it!

There are many amazing resources online for crocheter – in fact, there is quite a huge community of web pages and forums where users can share their tips and tricks. This is a great way to discover ore about your new skill, whilst meeting new people from all over the world and making friends. Once you have the ability to crochet, you won't look back!

Before you start crocheting, you have to take into account a series of tips that will make your life as a weaver much easier than you think. As you go above the needles and find a position that is comfortable for you to wear the strand when knitting, you will gradually relax, let go of the knitting, and find your own "tension of weaver."

When you start crocheting, it is often so overwhelming that the wool escapes between your fingers, the needles are drained, and the stitches are released while crocheting. This insecurity that causes us to face something new makes us weave the point very tightly. It's totally normal for this to happen, and you don't have to get overwhelmed or give it a lot of importance. You're not going to weave that tight always.

But until that happens, it is advisable to start crocheting with the right needles. So, what are the right needles when you start? The first thing you should know is that there are no good needles or bad needles in themselves. In principle, each type of needle is designed for a type of fiber and a type of weaver.

But when you start for the first time, you have to keep in mind that the needles offer some resistance and make them "break" the stitches on them a bit. This will make it harder for you to slip the stitches of the needle and to escape it, giving you better control above what you are doing. And for this, the needles that offer more resistance are bamboo.

Therefore, when you start crocheting, it is good that you start with this type of needles, so you can knit more comfortably. But as you learn, it is ideal to try different types of needles.

The first time you are going to try, and since you have never done it until now, your first instinct is a color that you can combine well with your clothes. I don't know why this happens, but the first thing that comes to mind is to choose dark wool (black, brown, navy blue, etc.), thinking that we can give more use to what we are going to weave because we can combine it better with our closet bottom.

I hope this was able to give you the inspiration you need to start crocheting, and that you take the skills you have learned here and show them off to the world. As with any new craft, practice makes perfect, and the more you work at this, the better you are going to become.

Have fun and please...leave me an honest review!

CPSIA information can be obtained
at www.ICGtesting.com
Printed in the USA
LVHW080805261020
669801LV00007B/921